Word POWER

What Every Educator Needs To Know About Teaching Vocabulary

by Steven Stahl
and Barbara Kapinus

NEA PROFESSIONAL LIBRARY

Copyright © 2001
National Education Association of the United States

Printing History:
First Printing: June 2001
Second Printing: August 2005
Third Printing: December 2006

Note: The opinions in this publication should not be construed as representing the policy or position of the National Education Association. Materials published by the NEA Professional Library are intended to be discussion documents for educators who are concerned with specialized interests of the profession.

Library of Congress Cataloging-in-Publication Data
Stahl, Steven A.
    Word power: what every educator needs to know about teaching vocabulary / by Steven Stahl and Barbara Kapinus.
    p. cm. — (The success in reading series)
"An NEA Professional Library publication."
ISBN 0-8106-2050-2
    1. Vocabulary—Study and teaching (Elementary) 2. Vocabulary—Study and teaching (Secondary) I. Kapinus, Barbara A. II. Title. III. Series.

LB1574.5 S73 2001
428.1'071'2—dc21

2001026614

Dedication

The authors dedicate this book to Isabel Beck, whose research inspired their work in this area, and whose mentoring and advice have helped them immeasurably. We would also like to thank our respective spouses, Kay and Bert, for their support and encouragement.

About the Authors

Steven A. Stahl, who died in 2004, was Professor of Reading Education at the University of Georgia where he directed the Reading Clinic. He was also Co-Director of the Center for the Improvement of Early Reading Achievement (CIERA). Steve received his doctorate in reading education from the Harvard Graduate School of Education. He worked as a public school teacher in Maine and New York. He published more than 100 books, monographs, articles, and book chapters. Steven had a long-standing interest in vocabulary instruction and its relationship to reading comprehension.

Barbara Kapinus is presently a senior policy analyst and education consultant at the National Education Association. Barbara has been the Director of the Curriculum and Instructional Improvement Program at the Council of Chief State School Officers, Specialist for Reading and Communication Skills at the Maryland State Department of Education, and, for 16 years in Prince George's County Public Schools, a classroom teacher, reading specialist, and curriculum specialist. She has published articles and book chapters on a range of reading-related topics. Barbara received her doctorate in reading from the University of Maryland at College Park. She has had a continuing interest in vocabulary instruction, and is convinced it is a key to clear thinking as well as effective communication.

Steven Stahl and Barbara Kapinus met at the National Reading Conference after presentations on vocabulary research. Prior to his death, they collaborated in vocabulary research, conference presentations, and authoring an article. While both Barbara and Steve pursued other aspects of reading, they maintained an interest in vocabulary and hoped that this book would spark vocabulary interest in teachers and students.

Word Power

Table of Contents

Introduction 7
    Who Can Use This Book 8
    How To Use This Book 9

Chapter 1: Learning Words and Their Meanings 11
    Wide Reading 11
        Choice Reading 11
        Reading Millionaires 12
        Book Leaves 12
        Read to Children 12
    Vocabulary Instruction 13
        Deciding Which Words To Teach 13
        Deciding How To Teach Words 14
            Ownership 14
            Multiple Encounters 14
            Using Definitional and Contextual Information 16
            Providing Definitional Information 17
            Providing Contextual Information 19
            Involving Students Actively 20

Chapter 2: Learning How To Learn Words 25
    Vocabulary Activities 25
        Definition Diagram 25
        Building Word Cards 27
        Creating Vocabulary Notebooks 27
        Letting Students Choose Vocabulary 27
        Using Dictionaries Effectively 28
    Understanding Word Parts 29
        Making New Words 29
        Using Prefixes and Roots To Understand Words 29
        Using Suffixes 29

Chapter 3: Learning About Words 33
Instructional Strategies 33
Semantic Feature Analysis 34
Question Connections 34
Thumbs Up or Down 35
Multiple Meaning Vocabulary 35

Conclusion 36

References 37

Other Resources 39
Books 39
Web Sites 39
Organizations 40

Introduction

Words are ubiquitous! From the moment students wake up until they turn in for the night, they're surrounded with spoken and written words. Their ability to understand and use these words with ease will, in large part, help determine their academic success. That's why it's so important that every student have as broad a vocabulary as possible. Vocabulary is strongly related to many important aspects of life, from reading comprehension to future salary. A student who knows the meanings of more words understands more of what he or she reads, from history to science to mathematics to music. If we teach our students the words, we give them the world!

We all remember the old way we learned word meanings. We looked them up, studied them for a test on Friday, and promptly forgot them. Unfortunately, many teachers continue to use the same approach. This is a mistake. The old dictionary exercises are largely ineffective in helping children learn word meanings. More effective approaches are the proven strategies in this book that help students develop deeper understandings— an "ownership"—of the meanings of words. When a student "owns" a word, it's readily available for speaking and writing, and the meaning is instantly accessed when listening or reading.

Think, too, of how much students' daily lives are enhanced when they develop a deep understanding and ownership of words such as "economy," "environment," "bias," "collaboration," "respect," "system," and "organic." These words frame broad, important topics both in and outside of the classroom. Truly comprehending the concepts behind these words leads students to a better understanding of topics in the daily news and the information in their own textbooks.

The research of Isabel Beck and her colleagues in the 1980s laid a solid base for this book, which includes some of the activities she used in her studies as well as ideas based on her findings. The strategies in this book were chosen not only for their effectiveness but also their efficiency—they don't require a great deal of time and planning—and their potential for being enjoyable and challenging. We've used the activities in classrooms and have received positive feedback from teachers who have tried them.

We've seen the need for vocabulary resources in our work with students and teachers. Several years ago, we interviewed students on how they learn vocabulary. We asked students how they recognized if they really knew and understood a word. Most students responded that they knew a word if they could define it or supply it on a vocabulary test. One student stood out, however. She responded that she was certain she knew a word when she could use it talking with friends or family or when writing for school. She was on the right track. Instruction that goes beyond assigning words and their definitions as preparation for a test carries the message that knowing a word means being able to use or think about it in a variety of ways. Hopefully, this book will help students and teachers understand what it means to know a word and some interesting ways to learn words.

WHO CAN USE THIS BOOK

Every teacher is a teacher of vocabulary. Whether you're teaching geometric terms in third grade math, literature in fifth grade, ecology in seventh grade science, governmental bodies in high school social studies, or even music terms, every content area has vocabulary to master. This book will help you:

- Challenge your students as they think about word meanings.
- Involve your students more actively in word learning.
- Increase the vocabulary and content understanding of your students.
- Guide your students toward the deep understanding and appreciation of words that comes from thoughtful learning rather than rote memorization.

INTRODUCTION

HOW TO USE THIS BOOK

The learning strategies described in this book will help your students develop thinking skills that involve analysis, comparison and contrast, organization of information, and application of information. These strategies can be used with students of all levels and can be combined and adapted in a wide variety of ways. The strategies invite creative and critical thinking about content and concepts.

We encourage teachers to use this book in any way that suits them. Some might want to read it through to the end and then decide how to use some of the strategies. Others might prefer to glance through the book until they see an activity to try. Rather than a prescribed sequence of activities, this book provides a set of possible tools that teachers can use, adapt, or choose to disregard if the utility of a specific approach is not immediately relevant.

However you decide to use the activities, your vocabulary development program will be more complete if you address three goals of vocabulary learning: learning words and their meanings, learning how to learn words, and learning about words. The next three chapters in this book address these goals and how to achieve them:

- **Learning Words and Their Meanings:** Chapter 1 suggests ways to enhance vocabulary through reading. It gives guidelines to help teachers decide which words to directly address with instruction, offers four principles for effective vocabulary instruction, and describes activities for helping students learn words.

- **Learning How To Learn Words:** Chapter 2 describes strategies that students can eventually use on their own as they take charge of their own vocabulary development.

- **Learning About Words:** Chapter 3 discusses strategies to help students understand how words function in communication and figurative language, so that students are truly able to know—and own—a word.

> One forgets words as one forgets names. One's vocabulary needs constant fertilizing or it will die.
> —Evelyn Waugh

chapter 1
Learning Words and Their Meanings

Children learn words in a variety of ways—from hearing, speaking, reading, writing, and instruction. Once students are reading fluently, they are likely to learn most of their new vocabulary through frequent and varied reading. Think of all the words you learned simply from reading. Studies have found that children learn anywhere from 1,000 to 5,000 new words per year, some from instruction, but largely from reading.

In this chapter, we review reading and vocabulary instruction strategies that teachers can use to enhance their students' word power.

WIDE READING

Research indicates that one powerful way for students to learn words and build vocabulary is to read frequently and widely. Students become familiar with new words by encountering them repeatedly as they read. The following activities give students an opportunity to read frequently.

Choice Reading
Students should have some time during the day to read books of their own choosing, particularly in elementary school. Choice reading can be scheduled for individual

classrooms or for the entire school at a certain time each day. Choice reading can be a silent activity, as in Sustained Silent Reading (SSR). During SSR, students read a book they have chosen for a specified time (usually at least 20 minutes). Younger children who are not yet able to read on their own may instead "pretend read" (point out pictures, make up stories, etc.) in pairs. The important thing is to provide time for children to read books of their choice. The following guidelines for teachers will help make this activity a success:

- Make books that cover a range of topics, formats, and reading levels available in classrooms where students participate in choice reading.

- Model reading and how important it is by reading your own book while students read theirs.

- Help students who are struggling with reading find something to read during choice reading. Guide more advanced readers toward appropriate texts as well.

- Take time at the end of choice reading to let students tell about their books. Pick a few students to share each time.

- Occasionally share something about your own reading.

Reading Millionaires

In this schoolwide reading program, children (and parents) keep logs of how many minutes they read outside of school. Outside reading can be done at home, in an afterschool program, or before school. These minutes are accumulated across the school, graphed, and celebrated when the entire school reaches 1,000,000 minutes. Celebrations could include throwing a pizza party, giving a book to each child who participated, or holding a reading "lock-in" (school sleepover). This activity involves a schoolwide effort of sending out logs, counting minutes read by class and by school, and keeping the graph current. But it's worthwhile.

Book Leaves

Another successful approach to reading involves counting the number of books that children read outside of school. One school we visited has a large construction-paper tree in the front lobby. Construction-paper leaves dot the tree, each with a child's name and a title of a book he or she has read. After a child reads a book, either during choice reading or after school, the child retells the story to a teacher or another adult. This entitles the child to put a leaf on the tree. Of course, instead of leaves, a school could use fish, bumblebees, birds, book characters, or monsters. The tree we saw was in full foliage, evidence of a school that reads.

Read to Children

For younger children, even those in kindergarten, storybooks are a valuable source of new vocabulary. Research shows that even very young children show marked differences in their knowledge of word meanings after listening to stories. When you read to young children, stop and discuss the meanings of some of the words, ones that you feel will be useful. You should not stop so much that children lose the thread of the story, but just enough to think about or play with words. Talking with students about some new and interesting words from a story is a great follow-up after reading. It can enhance comprehension as well as build vocabulary.

VOCABULARY INSTRUCTION

Although students learn the majority of the words they know through wide reading and everyday oral communications, it's important to teach some words directly. As we suggest below, some words are not likely to become part of one's vocabulary without direct instruction. In addition, effective vocabulary instruction helps students understand what they must do and know in order to learn new words on their own. As a consequence, vocabulary instruction must go beyond assigning students rote activities so that students achieve vocabulary growth and success in communicating.

Planning effective instruction in vocabulary requires careful decisions on what and how to teach. The sections below offer some ideas for determining both.

Deciding Which Words To Teach

Determining which words to teach is relatively simple for teachers of subjects such as mathematics, science, and social studies. These words are the critical concepts for understanding the content and mastering the processes in the subject areas. For English or language arts teachers, the decision is not always as clear. The following categories for words can provide guidance in that decision.

Words that students encounter as they read and learn tend to fall into three basic groups:

- ***Basic, high frequency words*** such as "cat," "house," and "green." Students may need some instruction on how to recognize these words when they read, but they will know the meanings.

- ***Extremely low frequency words*** with very specific application, such as "legato," "nova," and "crustacean." The most efficient way of dealing with these words is probably as they are needed for a specific passage, lesson, or content area unit.

- ***Sophisticated words*** frequently encountered and employed by mature, informed language users, such as "consistent," "representative," and "fluency."

Content area teachers should focus on the second tier, the low-frequency words with specific application. Language arts and English teachers should make sophisticated words the center of their vocabulary instruction.

Deciding How To Teach Words

As teachers plan vocabulary instruction, they will find that students are more interested and motivated when instruction is an integral part of classroom activities rather than an addendum that gets little attention. Research suggests that the following four principles can make instruction both effective and interesting:

1. Good vocabulary instruction **helps children gain ownership of words**, instead of just learning them well enough to pass a test.

2. Good vocabulary instruction **provides multiple exposures** through rich and varied activities to meaningful information about the word.

3. Good vocabulary instruction **includes both definitional and contextual information** about each word's meaning.

4. Good vocabulary instruction **involves children more actively** in word learning.

Good vocabulary instruction involves talking about words and making them a part of the fabric of your class. You can sneak vocabulary instruction into the times between activities—after a lesson and before lunch, during an impromptu class discussion, or as part of a planned curriculum. Good vocabulary instruction can be woven into the fabric of the entire school day. Like a strong thread, it will strengthen learning.

Here are some ways to apply the four principles for effective vocabulary instruction.

Ownership

In order for a word to be "owned," the word and its meaning must be readily available for communicating. Far too many students and teachers believe that getting a word or definition correct on a quiz constitutes knowing a word. As noted in the Introduction, however, when a student can use a new word in conversation or writing, he or she truly knows or owns that word. Instruction that goes beyond assigning words and their definitions as preparation for a test carries the message that knowing a word means being able to use or think about it in a variety of ways.

This ready availability or ownership comes only when the word has been actively used or processed several times and in many different ways. Students will then understand the conceptual information behind the word: that is, a word's definition, as well as information about examples and how the word is used. Active processing that uses a range of thinking skills promotes ownership. In fact, all of the activities in this book promote ownership.

Multiple Encounters

Since owning a word involves understanding several aspects of the word and the concept it represents, it's important that vocabulary instruction provide opportunities to encounter words in several ways and repeatedly. Often teachers simply use the same assignments for vocabulary each week, and vocabulary learning does not last much beyond the weekly test. Word Pairs, the activity described below, is one way to make students think about a word more than once. You can use this activity to review older words or newer words in a variety of ways.

Word Pairs. Give students pairs of words they have been studying in a chart like the one below. Ask them to check what they believe the relationship is between the two words. There might even be more than one relationship. Students can do this step in pairs or independently. It is a good homework assignment since students can usually do it independently, and it does not take long to complete.

The best part of this activity is the discussion of the relationships with the entire class. Students begin to see new relationships and consider the meaning of words at different levels. For example, "opposites" often also have a "go-together" relationship. "Warmth" might be the opposite of "coolness," but it is also a point along a continuum that both share. This activity offers students the opportunity to do some critical thinking and enjoy a discussion about words. For example, the word pair "satellite-star," at first consideration, would appear to go together since they are both celestial bodies. However, stars tend to be the center of celestial movement, while satellites move in orbit around other celestial bodies. Consequently, some might argue that they are opposites. This is the kind of deeper thinking that discussions of word pairs can promote.

Word Pairs is also an effective way to review words studied previously since those words can be paired with new words. In content classes, such as science and social studies, the activity provides an opportunity to build on, link with, and extend concepts learned earlier.

	Same	**Opposite**	**Go Together**	**No Relation**
Desert-nomad			X	
Nomad-wanderer	X			
Nomad- settler		X		
Desert-city				X
Star-energy			X	
Satellite-star		X	X	

Anticipation Guides. Another activity that might be useful in providing multiple encounters is to have children rate their knowledge of words prior to reading a story. This calls their attention to the words while they are reading and sets them up for learning more about the words. This can be followed up with post-reading instruction.

	Know the word well	Have heard of it	Know nothing about the word
mayor		X	
proclamation		X	
piñata			X
canasta			X
electrician	X		
knish			X

Using Definitional and Contextual Information

When children "know" a word, they not only know the word's definition and its logical relationship with other words (such as synonyms, antonyms, categories, and examples), they also know how that word functions in different contexts. For example, consider the word "history." Its definition might be something like "a record of the past." However, "history" refers to distinctly different things in the following sentences:

1. He enjoyed reading about the early *history* of America.

2. She had a class in *history* right after lunch.

3. They had a *history* of helping their neighbors.

4. That way of doing things is *history*.

These all fit under the general definition of "history," but the meaning varies according to the context of each sentence. The first refers to a particular era in time, the second to a course of study, the third to a personal record, and the last to a condition.

The subtle changes that a word's "meaning" goes through when it interacts with other information in context may explain why definitions are so difficult to use in learning word meanings. In one study, researchers asked children to read definitions of words and then to make sentences that fit the definitions for those words. The children's sentences often showed serious misunderstandings of the definitions. For example, after seeing the following definition:

redress—set right, repair, remedy; when King Arthur tried to redress wrongs in his kingdom,

one student wrote, "The redress for getting well [when] you're sick is to stay in bed." Another student, seeing that erode means "to eat away," wrote, "My family erodes often." Even though these sentences seem funny, they suggest that a word's "meaning" is not captured fully in the dictionary definition. Instead, a word's meaning needs to be seen in context, so that the learner can see how it relates to other words in conventional spoken or written context.

It helps to give students additional definitional information. For example, "redress" is usually used to mean repairing something a person or group has done that is wrong or has a bad effect: "The boy's father tried to redress the boy's rudeness by having him apologize." Additional definitional information for "erode" would refer to things wearing away: "The wind and waves eroded the beach until it was almost gone."

Better definitions are only part of the solution. Using dictionaries or glossaries alone to learn word meanings does not seem to be an effective approach to learning words. The research shows that approaches that provide only definitional information *do not* significantly affect children's reading comprehension. In contrast, methods that provide both definitional and contextual information *do* significantly improve comprehension. Such methods include providing a definition for a word and discussing how the definition fits into two or more sentences containing that word, or having children write and discuss several sentences for each new word. Semantic Mapping (page 21) and Possible Sentences (page 19), two strategies described later in this book, will help students think about both definitional and contextual information.

Providing Definitional Information

Information about the relationship between new and known words is an important part of word learning. Here are some ways to provide definitional information that make use of that relationship.

Use Synonyms. It's useful to discuss how two or more synonyms differ. For example, "debris," "trash," and "garbage" are synonyms, but have subtly different meanings. "Trash" is a more general term for things that are left over, such as paper, tree limbs, bottle caps, and unwanted mail. Although they are treated synonymously, the preferred usage for "garbage" is organic matter, such as leftovers from dinner. "Debris" refers to trash generated by an event, such as an accident or an outdoor concert. A discussion of all three words would generate strong connections among the words, as well as the ability to begin drawing on the subtle differences in connotation.

Use Antonyms. An antonym is a word that shares all but one feature with the target word. For example, the opposite of "love" is "hate" because both "love" and "hate" are strong emotions, but one is positive and one is negative. Not all words have antonyms. A word like "magician" doesn't. Discussing which words come the closest as antonyms for these words focuses the student on the important features of a word's meaning.

Use Examples and Nonexamples. In order to develop a clear understanding of words that represent new concepts, students need to consider nonexamples as well as examples of the word. For example, people who live in a group that moves from place to place and does not consider one place home are referred to as nomads. A businesswoman who travels a great deal but has a place she considers home is not referred to as a nomad.

Use Concept Maps. A concept map is a tool to visually organize information about a word. Take a look at the concept map below. Choose a word you want to define. Through class discussion, generate information for the categories. For "What is this?" ask students what group or category the word belongs to. For example, a pachyderm is an animal with a tough hide. For "What is it like?" have students generate descriptions that stress various characteristics of a pachyderm. For example, students might say that pachyderms are usually large.

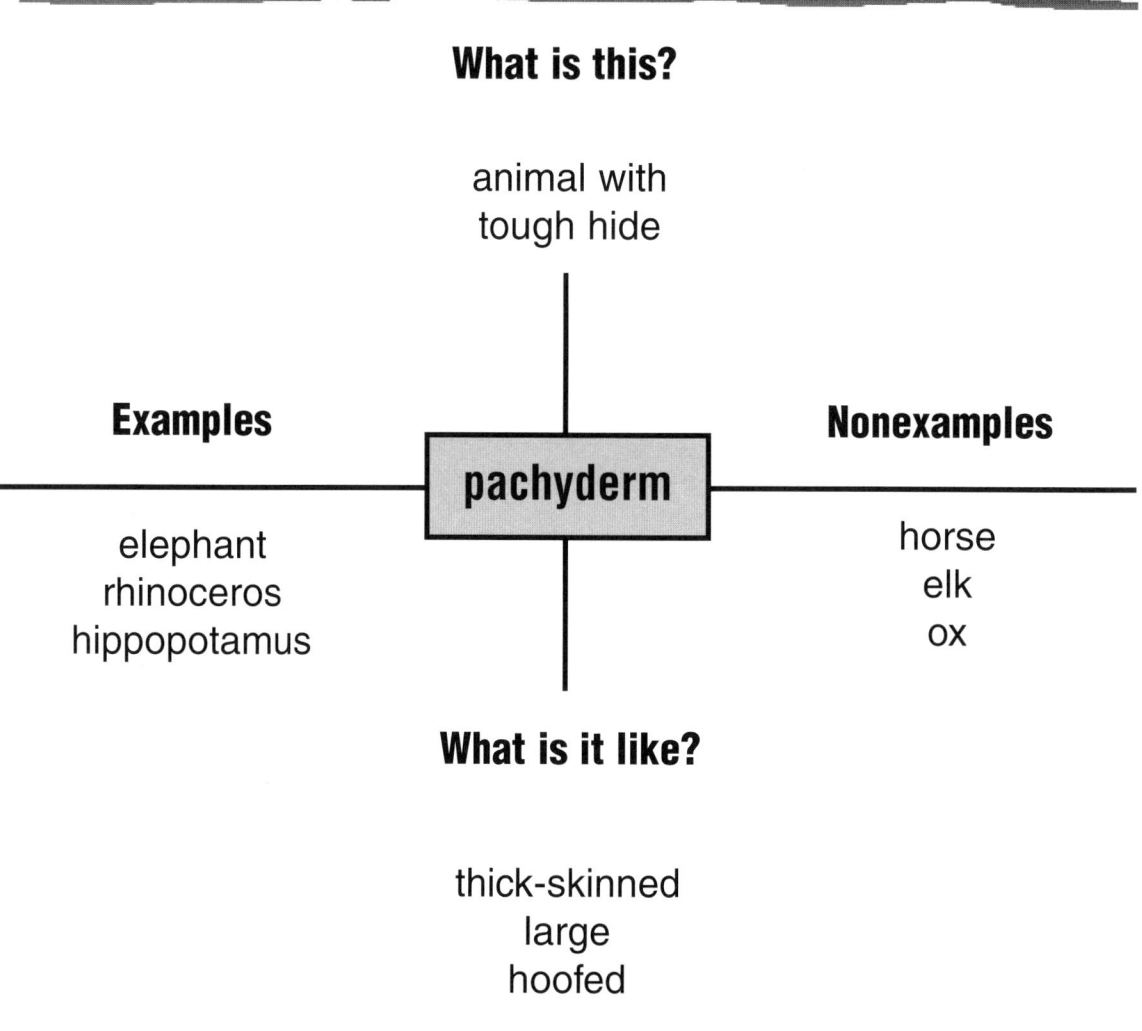

LEARNING WORDS AND THEIR MEANINGS

Providing Contextual Information

Effective vocabulary instruction also provides children with exposure to words in context. This may vary from the traditional approach of discussing the meaning of the word in a sentence from a story or passage to the three activities listed below.

Context Comparisons. Use a series of sentences to discuss the meaning of a word. Put two or three sentences on the blackboard. You may have to provide a synonym for the word. Have students compare and contrast how the word is used in the sentences, bringing up commonalities and differences in the different contexts. For example:

1. Jane is a *maverick* whose opinions often differ from the rest of the group.

2. That person is a *maverick* and you cannot count her vote.

3. He has a *maverick* tuft of hair on the crown of his head.

4. The tan kitten is a *maverick* who is always wandering off.

Scenarios. Make up a scenario for a new word, drawing a verbal picture of the concept. For "humiliation," for example, you might describe a situation in which someone was humiliated. Younger children may draw a real picture.

Possible Sentences. This approach not only encourages students to pay attention to new words in a passage they are reading, but it also increases students' motivation and engagement in reading. Here are the steps of this strategy:

Prereading

1. Introduce the topic of the passage and discuss what students already know about it.

2. List key words from the passage. These are words the students are not likely to know that are explained implicitly or explicitly in the passage.

3. Have students offer possible sentences containing the words. Students should use the information they already have about the topic to help themselves in this activity.

During Reading

Have students read their sentences and decide whether the sentences are reasonable based on the information provided by the passage.

After Reading

1. As a group (or first in small groups, then as an entire class), evaluate the reasonableness of the sentences and revise them if necessary.

2. Generate new sentences using the words from the original list. Students might do this in pairs or triads before sharing as a class.

3. Make up sentences containing two or more words from the list of words to be taught. Some classes really enjoy making sentences with all of the words. For a six-word list, this can be challenging.

Involving Students Actively

The fourth principle of effective vocabulary instruction relates to how active students are at constructing links between new information and already known information. Children remember more information when they are actively relating it to known information, transforming it in their own words, generating examples and nonexamples, and thinking of antonyms and synonyms.

Students can be asked to process information about words at three levels:

1. They can use information at a rote level by simply memorizing the connection between a word and its definition.

2. They can process a word by comprehending it when they read it or by using the definitional information to find an antonym or classify the word.

3. They can generate new associations by putting a definition into their own words, generating a sentence using the word, or making new connections between the word and other concepts or new connotations. This level involves taking the "meaning" of the word and doing something further with it.

The important thing for teachers to remember is that the degree to which students are engaged in the third level of processing (known as generative) affects their retention of the word and its meaning. Therefore teachers should offer students many opportunities to communicate their own understandings of words. The three strategies below help students become more actively involved with learning words.

Active Discussion. Discussion adds an important dimension to vocabulary instruction. In order to participate in a discussion, children must practice or prepare a response themselves while waiting to be called upon. This practiced response appears to lead to learning. Because a student's expectation of being called on is an important part of this process, teachers should allow all students in the class some "think" time before calling on one individual. Also, a teacher should be sensitive to his or her patterns of calling on students and avoid just calling on the "fast" students. If students don't think they will be called on, they will not practice a response. Without the practiced response, discussion is not as valuable a learning experience.

Discussion seems to improve vocabulary learning in general. Students benefit not only from the active processing that takes place when they participate in discussions, but also from the contributions of other children. It's our experience that children who enter a vocabulary lesson without any knowledge of a target word learn a great deal from their peers, who may have partial or even fairly good knowledge of the word. In open discussions, children are often able to construct a good idea of a word's meaning from the partial knowledge of the class as a whole. Sometimes, however, we had to interject some information about the word, such as a quick definition.

Asking students to share their responses with a partner before sharing with the entire class involves more students in classroom discussions. Also, asking students to repeat the responses of the students before them, and then give their own responses, is another way for teachers to help students listen to the ideas of their peers.

Semantic Mapping. Active discussion is also an important element of semantic mapping, a strategy that uses graphic representations to show the connections between words. Semantic mapping is a very popular method for teaching vocabulary because it's highly adaptable to all grade levels, content areas, and instructional situations. Semantic mapping can be used with advanced topics, such as high school economics, or simple topics, such as a kindergarten lesson on farm animals. Many approaches to semantic mapping have been developed over the years, and most use the same general procedure described below.

Brainstorming

1. Begin with a topic, such as weather. Have students think of words that go with that topic. List the words on one half of the blackboard.

2. As the discussion progresses, integrate the to-be-learned words into that topic. If, for example, you want to add "anemometer," you might ask if anyone knows the instrument that measures the speed of wind. If no one does, then provide the word.

3. Proceed until you have added all of the words you want to teach, making sure to discuss each word briefly as you add it to the board.

Developing the Map

1. Draw a circle with the topic in the middle on the other half of the blackboard.

2. Have students come up with some categories for the brainstormed words. Make a circle for each category, connected to the central topic circle.

3. Have the students add the brainstormed words to the category circles, making sure all words are included.

4. Add a blank category circle, to be used after reading.

WORD POWER

Reading the Selection and Follow-Up

1. Have the students read the selection, either silently, in pairs, or however they usually read in class. If you teach younger children, you can read to the class.

2. Discuss what concepts were included in the selection. Add additional terms to the semantic map from the text.

3. Ask if there were other categories included in the selection. Add a category to the blank circle, with related terms.

Discussion seems to be a crucial element in the effectiveness of semantic mapping. This is especially true for the children who begin with lower vocabularies. High vocabulary children already know most of the related words, which helps them to reinforce the target words. Semantic mapping helps children with low vocabularies *learn* the related words along with the target words. The resulting map might look like this:

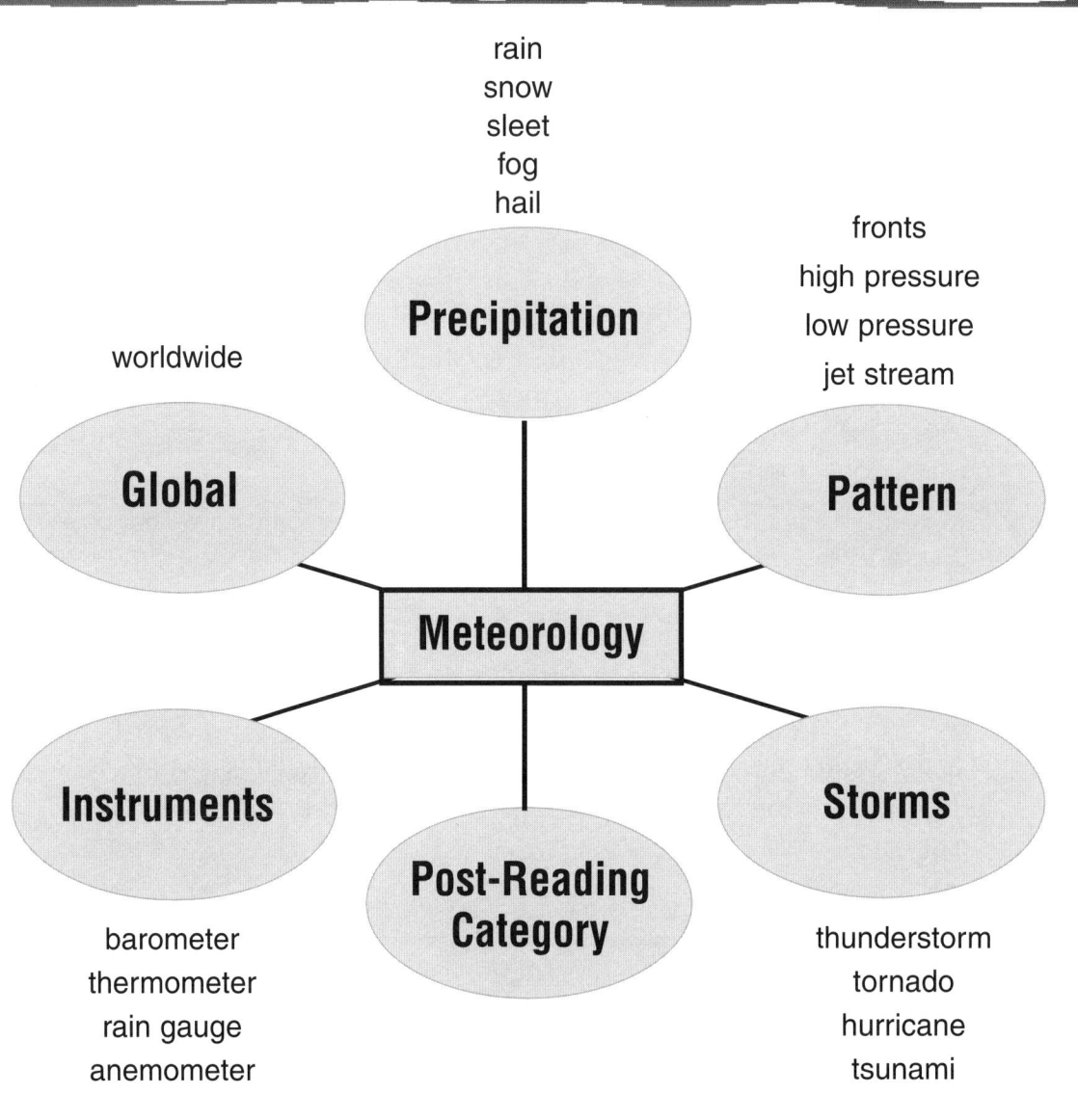

LEARNING WORDS AND THEIR MEANINGS

Four-Square Vocabulary. This is a quick activity that teaches a few words from a to-be-read story. It uses the following six steps to discuss examples and nonexamples and then generate a definition.

1. Have students take a sheet of paper and fold it into four quadrants.

2. In the upper left box, dictate the word that is to be taught, for example, "soothing."

3. Describe the word. You might say, "when something is soothing, it makes you feel relaxed."

4. Have students give you examples of that concept. For "soothing," students might provide "music," "a bath," or "a nap." Have students write four or five of these in the upper right box.

5. Next, have students provide nonexamples of the concept. For "soothing," students might say things that are not soothing, such as "tests," "loud noises," or "being called on by the teacher. " Have them write four or five nonexamples in the lower right box.

6. Finally, have students write a definition of the concept in the lower left box. Have them share these with the class. These definitions can also be incorporated into the students' Vocabulary Notebooks (page 27).

Soothing	**Music** **Bath** **Nap**
Comforting **Offering Relief**	**Tests** **Loud noises** **Being called on**

Word Wizard. Word Wizard can be a great follow-up to any vocabulary activity. Its purpose is to get children to notice words in their environment and to be sensitive to words they have learned in vocabulary lessons or heard in storybooks.

To prepare for this activity, the teacher hangs up a large graphic of a wizard (or any large chart or picture). Each student is assigned a vocabulary word. As a student hears or sees the word in context, either the student or the teacher writes the word and its context on a Post-It™ note and puts it on the chart. After a period of time (perhaps every two weeks or month), the student who has "found" the most words becomes the Word Wizard.

> Words are all we have.
> —*Samuel Beckett*

chapter 2

Learning How To Learn Words

As students move through school, their need to learn vocabulary continues. However, at some point, usually high school or college, teachers no longer directly address vocabulary but assume students will take responsibility for learning new words on their own.

VOCABULARY ACTIVITIES

The following six activities lay the foundation to help students gradually take charge of their own vocabulary development. The activities include making definition diagrams, building word cards, creating vocabulary notebooks, letting students choose the vocabulary list, using dictionaries effectively, and understanding word parts.

Definition Diagram

This activity is based on Aristotle's notion of definition. Aristotle believed that words could be defined in terms of a "genus" or category and "differentiae" or things that distinguish the word from other members of the category. This activity uses a diagram to structure a definition about a word. You can use this strategy in two ways—to teach general information about definitions or to teach specific words:

1. Prepare a blank diagram. Make sure each child has a copy of the same dictionary.

2. Begin with an already-known concept. "Computer" works well.

3. Discuss with students the parts of a definition—the category (What it is), the description (What it is like), examples, and nonexamples.

4. Discuss with students what information might fit into the categories for "computer."

   - What it is—Electronic device
   - What it is like—Box for CPU, keyboard, monitor
   - Examples—PC, Macintosh
   - Nonexamples—Television, stapler, brain

5. Have students choose words to look up in their dictionaries. Put each definition on the board. Discuss how the information in the dictionary definition fits into the diagram. Repeat this activity with four or five words.

6. Have students generate their own definitions, using the categories in the diagram.

Word	What it is	What it is like	Examples	Nonexamples
computer	electronic device	box for CPU, keyboard, monitor	PC Macintosh	television stapler brain
metropolis	city	large busy	New York City Los Angeles	village suburb mall

LEARNING HOW TO LEARN WORDS

Building Word Cards
This is an effective way for students to build their own personal word collections and a logical step in helping students become "wordophiles." Have students keep index cards with the information you see on the top right card.

WORD	
definitional information	contextual information
	personal clue

Take a look at the example on the bottom card to see what the definitional information, contextual information, and personal clue for the word "repeal" might look like on a student's index card.

REPEAL	
To withdraw or take back officially	The Senate decided to repeal skateboarding in the park.
	The city repealed its decision to hold a parade.

When students have made five to ten cards, they can use them to:

- Sort words into the parts of speech, e.g., nouns, verbs, adjectives, or adverbs.

- Find words that have certain connotations such as good and bad, desirable and undesirable, descriptive, etc.

- Make sentences with pairs of the words.

- Group the words and then explain the basis of the grouping.

Creating Vocabulary Notebooks
Vocabulary notebooks can be boring, or they can be a real source of fun and interesting learning. Rather than sterile collections of definitions, vocabulary notebooks should contain all sorts of information, including contexts (parts of stories, paragraphs, poems, songs) where the word appeared, pictures of the word, synonyms, and antonyms. Vocabulary notebooks can be electronic, using database programs, which would allow a great deal of flexibility in terms of what students could include.

Letting Students Choose Vocabulary
Teachers do not have to be the sole word choosers. You can open the choice of words to students, as they work in groups or individually. Groups or individuals can review the text that the class is reading and suggest words for the entire class to learn. Establish criteria for word selection, such as how important the word is to the story or chapter, how well the word can be understood from the context alone, and whether the word is useful outside of the story.

Using Dictionaries Effectively

Research has shown that traditional vocabulary instruction, in which students look up words in a dictionary, is not effective in improving comprehension. There are a number of reasons for this:

- Memorizing definitions does not require the student to make connections between the new word and already known information. Good vocabulary instruction requires a person to think actively about words in order to have ownership of them.

- A word's meaning is more than what is contained in a definition. Words subtly change in different contexts, rather than maintaining a strict "meaning."

- Children can have a difficult time understanding definitions. They often make judgments based on one part or another of the definition, missing the connotations of the word.

However, dictionaries are a useful adjunct to word learning, if used correctly. We suggest the following strategies.

- ***Use dictionaries after a student reads a word in context, rather than before.*** This is how adults use dictionaries. Instead of having children memorize words before reading, encourage them to use dictionaries while reading. This way they have the context and can use the definition to understand what the word means in that context.

- ***Teach students about dictionary definitions.*** Definitions usually contain a category for the defined word and how that word differs from other members of the category. Have students analyze dictionary definitions, picking out these elements within a definition. Also have them rewrite definitions in their own words.

- ***Try some nontraditional dictionaries.*** For example, the COBUILD English Dictionary (HarperCollins) defines words by using them in sentences. The COBUILD defines "exotic" with the sentence: "Something that is exotic is strange, unusual or interesting because it comes from a distant country." This is considerably more interesting than merely saying it means "foreign, strange, non-native." (See http://titania.cobuild.collins.co.uk for other examples.)

- ***Have fun with definitions.*** The Word of the Day on the Oxford English Dictionary Web site (http://www.oed.com/cgi/display/wotd) traces how words have been used through the years and gives the word in various contexts. Teachers can plan activities such as Word Wizard (page 24) around the Word of the Day, or it can be included in the school's morning announcements, and all students can be encouraged to use it that day.

UNDERSTANDING WORD PARTS

Knowledge of word parts greatly improves children's vocabulary. One estimate is that over half of all words have a recognizable prefix, suffix, or are a compound. Knowing "tele" means "far" unlocks "telephoto," "telephone," "television," and "teleprompter." Or knowing that "mnem" refers to memory could unlock not only "mnemonic," but also "amnesty" and "amnesia."

Of the most common word parts, prefixes are the easiest to teach, because they tend to have an easy-to-grasp meaning and are relatively common. They also are generative. Knowing "un" means "not," one could understand not only "uncommon" and "unusual," but also "Uncola®" and all kinds of other "uns."

Suffixes, on the other hand, are more difficult to teach, because they tend to mark a part of speech: for example, "-ment" is the "state of" as in "contentment," "advertisement," and "engagement." This can be difficult for young children to follow. Instead of being defined, suffixes should be used in context: "He showed his contentment by leaning back on his chair."

Making New Words

Teachers can have students add "un" to words to make new words; then they can put each new word into a sentence. For example:

Able	He was *unable* to meet you today.
Certain	The third grader was *uncertain* about the answer on the test.
Imaginative	The movie was boring and *unimaginative*.

Using Prefixes and Roots To Understand Words

Throughout history, when people need a new word, they often make them up using prefixes and roots. When Louis Deguerre developed a new approach to making pictures, he called it "photography" or "light" and "writing." Ask students to look at words like "photosynthesis," "telephoto," and "photocell" and think about how their meanings reflect the meanings of the prefixes and roots.

Using Suffixes

Suffixes often change the part of speech of a word, so that a noun can be used as an adverb, or an adjective can be used as a noun. Teachers can have students add suffixes to words so they sound right in a sentence. (Note: You may have to preteach the suffixes.) For example:

Move	He watched the *movement* of the tree as the breeze went through it.

Devil	Alison had a _devilish_ streak in her that made her do mischief.
Sleep	Carly was a sound _sleeper_. Nothing would wake her.
Selfish	Their _selfishness_ made them very unpopular.
Liberate	The people cheered for the _liberation_ of their city.
Free	After years in prison, _freedom_ felt good.

The following three charts show the most frequent prefixes and suffixes, other useful prefixes, and some common word roots.

THE MOST FREQUENT AFFIXES IN ENGLISH

Rank	Prefix	Percent of all prefixed words	Suffix	Percent of all suffixed words
1	un-	26	-s, -es	31
2	re-	14	-ed	20
3	in-, im-, il-, ir- (not)	11	-ing	14
4	dis-	7	-ly	7
5	en-, em-	4	-er, -or (agent)	4
6	non-	4	-ion, -tion, -ation, -ition	4
7	in-, im- (in)	3	-able, -ible	2
8	over-	3	-al, -ial	1
9	mis-	3	-y	1
10	sub-	3	-ness	1
11	pre-	3	-ity, -ty	1
12	inter-	3	-ment	1
13	fore-	3	-ic	1
14	de-	2	-ous, -eous, ious	1
15	trans-	2	-en	1
16	super-	1	-er (comparative)	1
17	semi-	1	-ive, -ative, -tive	1
18	anit-	1	-ful	1
19	mid-	1	-less	1
20	under-	1	-est	1
	All others	3	All others	7

From White, Sowell, and Yanagihara (1989)

NUMBER AND TIME PREFIXES

mono-	one	monocular, monocle, monk, monarch, monaural
uni-	one	unicycle, uniform, unicorn, unique, unisex
bi-	two	bicycle, biped, bipartisan, binocular, bivalve, bimonthly, bilingual
di-	two	dichotomy, dilemma, diphthong, diurnal
duo-, da	two	duet, dual, duo, duplicate
tri-	three	triangle, triple, tripod, tricycle
quad-	four	quadrilateral, quart, quarter, quartet, quadruped
quint-	five	quintuplet
penta-	five	pentagon, pentatonic, pentameter
sex-	six	sexagenarian, sextant
hexa-	six	hexagon, hexagram, hexameter
sept-	seven	September, septet
hepta-	seven	heptagon
octa, octo-	eight	octopus, octagon, October, octet, octogenarian, octane
non, novem-	nine	November, nonagon, nonagenarian
dec-	ten	decade, decathlon, December, decimal, decaliter
centi-	hundred	century, centennial, cent, centigrade, centimeter
milli-	thousand	millipede, millenium, milligram, millimeter
kilo-	thousand	kilogram, kilometer
And time prefixes...		
ante	before	antecedent, anteroom, antebellum
post-	after	postwar, postpartum

COMMON WORD ROOTS

Root	Meaning	Origin	Examples
aud	hear	Latin	audible, auditory
astro	star	Greek	astronomy, astrophysics, astrology
bio	life	Greek	biology, biosphere
dict	speak, tell	Latin	dictate, predict, dictator
geo	earth	Greek	geology, geography
meter	measure	Greek	thermometer, barometer
min	little, small	Latin	minimum, minimal
mit, mis	send	Latin	mission, transmit, remit, missile
ped	foot	Latin	pedestrian, pedal, pedestal
phon	sound	Greek	phonograph, microphone
port	carry	Latin	transport, portable, import
scrib, script	write	Latin	scribble, manuscript, inscription
spect	see	Latin	inspect, spectator, respect
struct, instruct	build, form	Latin	construction, destruct, instruct

To call forth a concept, a word is needed.
—Antoine Laurent Lavoisier

chapter 3
Learning About Words

Learning words and their meanings, as well as learning how to learn words on their own, will help students become proficient language users. However, they will become truly powerful language users only when they understand how words function in communication, the subtle connotations of words, and even their origins. Students will become powerful language users who can pick the best words to convey ideas, inspire actions, express feelings, evoke emotions, heal wounds, make peace, and connect with others. Powerful language users are thoughtful as well as knowledgeable. They can consider not only the meaning of words, but also their appropriateness, value, and potential effects.

INSTRUCTIONAL STRATEGIES

Students need to think more deeply about word meaning, how words relate to each other, and different ways to consider words. The activities in this section challenge students' thinking and enable them to gain insights into the meanings and uses of words. Because the activities require thinking but not a lot of writing, students tend to find them entertaining. Teachers can preserve the climate of fun in these activities by encouraging students to think in divergent ways about words and honoring divergent but reasonable interpretations of words and how they relate to each other.

Semantic Feature Analysis

This activity is especially effective in content area classes such as social studies, history, and geography. The teacher asks the students to consider a word and to analyze examples of the concept. Follow the steps below:

1. Develop a chart like the one below for the concept, examples, and characteristics. In this case, the vocabulary words relate to the concept of transportation.

2. Have students check the characteristics that apply for each example. They can do this in pairs.

3. Go through the examples and discuss the characteristics the students marked. This can bring out some lively discussion. For example, students might not think that camels use fuel at first but, upon consideration, realize that food is fuel. Then a follow-up question might be whether all forms of transportation use some sort of fuel.

	Air	Land	Water	Wheels	Motors / Engines	Carry Cargo	Use Fuel
Car		X		X	X	X	X
Airplane	X	X	X	X	X	X	X
Ship			X		X	X	X
Train		X		X	X	X	X
Bicycle		X		X		X	X
Camel		X				X	X
Gondola			X			X	X
Caravan		X		X	X	X	X

Question Connections

Make up questions for a list of words by using the words in pairs. For "actuary," "herbalist," "hermit," and "accountant," you might make up sentences like "Can an *actuary* be an *accountant*?" "Can an *actuary* be a *herbalist*?" "Can a *hermit* be a *herbalist*?" "Can a *hermit* be an *actuary*?" "Can a *hermit* be *amorous*?" and so on. Discuss why or why not. The questions could be serious as well. This is a great way to review past words by using them in the questions. For example, "Can a *monarchy* be a *democracy*?" " Does an *object in motion* have *inertia*?" "Can a *miser* be a *philanthropist*?" "Can a *whole number* be a *fraction*?" Have students discuss the reasons for their answers.

Thumbs Up or Down

For each word taught, read aloud a series of sentences. Have students say "Yay" if the word is used correctly or "Boo" if the word is used incorrectly (or give a thumbs up or thumbs down sign). Discuss students' opinions. As a variation of this activity, you can just say a word and not an entire sentence. Have students respond with a thumbs up, thumbs down, or thumbs sideways if the word carries a good, bad, or neutral connotation. For example, "erode" might be a thumbs down because it suggests rust or wearing away a resource such as soil; "energy" might be a thumbs up; and "satellite" might be a thumbs sideways. If this is done during a content class such as science, direct the students to use the meaning of the word that fits that context. The discussion of rationales behind the positive, negative, and neutral connotations is the heart of this activity and the part that challenges students' thinking.

Multiple Meaning Vocabulary

It's important to give some time to teaching students the multiple meanings of frequently encountered words. These are words with two or more distinctly different meanings. For example, "state" can mean a "place" (either real or metaphoric, like a state of mind) or it can mean "to say something." Below is a list of some words with multiple meanings.

Words with Multiple Meanings			
State	Measure	Plane	Press
Power	Match	Rear	Tack
Division	Cut	Rational	Prompt
Baste	Point	Solution	Air
Serve	Mark	Culture	Draw
Try	Check	Slant	Bound
Play	Foot	Stocks	Commercial
Fast	Line	Mission	Case
Clear	Set	Pitch	Leave

Have students use the Word Card strategy described previously on page 27 to keep track of the multiple meanings of those words. They can make a separate Word Card for each meaning of each word.

CONCLUSION

The best language users, the people who impress us or who are highly successful communicators, have a command of the meaning of words, powerful thinking skills for choosing and using words effectively, and a rich understanding of the connotations and denotations of words. These people have "word power." Teachers from kindergarten on up have a key role to play in arming students with word power for the rest of their lives. Through helping students to learn words and their meanings, learn how to learn words on their own, and appreciate words in all their subtleties, we are equipping students—and society—with a powerful tool.

Word power is not simply important for professional success. It's essential for the continued presence of a citizenry that understands and participates in the social and political processes that maintain civilization and culture. If the pen is indeed mightier than the sword, words are the power behind that might. One of the most important goals of education is to pass word power on to future citizens, leaders, and decision makers.

> A powerful agent is the right word.
> —*Mark Twain*

References

Anglin, J.M. 1993. Vocabulary Development: A Morphological Analysis. *Monographs of the Society for Research in Child Development*, Serial No. 238, 58 (10).

Beck, I.L., C.A. Perfetti, and M.G. McKeown. 1982. Effects of Long-Term Vocabulary Instruction on Lexical Access and Reading Comprehension. *Journal of Educational Psychology* 74: 506-521.

Blachowicz, C.L.Z., and P. Fischer. 2001. *Teaching Vocabulary in All Classrooms*. Columbus, Ohio: Merrill.

Dale, E., and J. O'Rourke. 1986. *Vocabulary Building*. Columbus, Ohio: Zaner-Bloser.

Dole, J.A., C. Sloan, and W. Trathen. 1995. Teaching Vocabulary Within the Context of Literature. *Journal of Reading* 38(6): 452-460.

Eads, M. and W. Cockrum. 1985. Teaching Word Meanings by Expanding Schemata vs. Dictionary Work vs. Reading in Context. *Journal of Reading* 28: 492-497.

Graves, M.F., and M.C. Prenn. 1986. Costs and Benefits of Various Methods of Teaching Vocabulary. *Journal of Reading* 29: 596-602.

Heimlich, J.E., and S.D. Pittelman. 1986. *Semantic Mapping: Classroom Applications.* Newark, Del.: International Reading Association.

Johnson, D.D. 2001. *Vocabulary in the Elementary and Middle School.* Boston: Allyn and Bacon.

Johnson, D.D., S. Toms-Bronowski, and S.D. Pittelman. 1982. *An Investigation of the Effectiveness of Semantic Mapping and Semantic Feature Analysis with Intermediate Grade Children,* Program Report 83-3. Madison, Wisc.: Wisconsin Center for Educational Research, University of Wisconsin.

McKeown, M.G. 1993. Creating Effective Definitions for Young Word Learners. *Reading Research Quarterly* 32: 184-200.

Nist, S.L., and S. Olejnik. 1995. The Role of Context and Dictionary Definitions on Varying Levels of Word Knowledge. *Reading Research Quarterly* 30: 172-193.

O'Masta, G., and J. Wolf. 1991. Encouraging Independent Reading Through the Reading Millionaires Project. *The Reading Teacher* 44: 656-662.

Schwartz, R.M., and T. Raphael. 1985. Concept of Definition: A Key to Improving Students' Vocabulary. *The Reading Teacher* 39: 98-203.

Scott, J.A., and W.E. Nagy. 1997. Understanding the Definitions of Unfamiliar Verbs. *Reading Research Quarterly* 32: 184-200.

Stahl. S.A. 1998. *Vocabulary Development.* Cambridge, Mass.: Brookline Press.

Stahl, S.A., and M.M. Fairbanks. 1986. The Effects of Vocabulary Instruction: A Model-Based Meta-Analysis. *Review of Educational Research* 56 (1): 72-110.

Stahl, S.A., and B.A. Kapinus. 1991. Possible Sentences: Predicting Word Meanings To Teach Content-Area Vocabulary. *The Reading Teacher* 45: 36-45.

Stahl, S.A., and S.J. Vancil. 1986. Discussion Is What Makes Semantic Maps Work. *The Reading Teacher* 40: 62-67.

White, T.G., J. Sowell, and A. Yanagihara. 1989. Teaching Elementary Students To Use Word-Part Clues. *The Reading Teacher* 42: 302-309.

RESOURCES

Other Resources

BOOKS

Johnson, Dale. 2000. *Vocabulary in the Elementary and Middle School.* Boston: Allyn and Bacon.
This book illustrates how to stimlate and expand vocabulary and language learning, with research-based analysis, activities, and other teaching aids.

Hartill, Marguerite. 1999. *Fab Vocab!* New York: Scholastic.
Vocabulary-building and reviewing activities include Acrostics With a Twist and Vocabulary Jeopardy, written by a fifth-grade teacher for grades 3 through 6.

Lipton, James. 1993. *An Exaltation of Larks: The Ultimate Edition.* New York: Penguin Putnam Inc.
Word-lovers in higher grades will enjoy this book, which describes and illustrates collective nouns (a leap of leopards, a parliament of owls) that have been used throughout history, as well as some that the author created.

Nickelson, Leann. 1999. *Quick Activities to Build a Very Voluminous Vocabulary* (Grades 4-8). New York: Scholastic.
Mini-lessons, graphic organizers, and other ready-to-use activities.

Robb, Laura. 1999. *Easy Mini-Lessons for Building Vocabulary.* New York: Scholastic. This book shows teachers ways to build vocabulary before, during, and after reading, in any subject area. The author, a Virginia language arts specialist, focuses on grades 4 through 8.

WEB SITES

Vocabulary University uses cartoons and puzzles to expand students vocabulary at www.vocabulary.com

Visitors can ask Dr. Dictionary a question about words and word usage, receive a Word-of-the-Day by E-mail and use many other resources at www.dictionary.com

The Oxford English Dictionary's Word-of-the-Day can be accessed by visiting www.oed.com/cgi/display/wotd

Many other dictionaries maintain Web sites. They include the COBUILD dictionary mentioned in the text (http://titania.cobuild.collins.co.uk); Merriam-Webster (www.m-w.com); and Random House Webster (www.randomhouse.com)

Teachers who work with students who are learning English as their second language will find some useful tips at Ohio State University's Web site, www.ohiou.edu/esl/english/vocabulary.html#ESP

NEA Works4Me Tips Library includes some suggestions from teachers on creative ways to teach spelling and vocabulary. View these tips at www.nea.org/helpfrom/growing/works4me/content/spelling.html

The Vocabulary Review is an online journal about how to use, and not use, words. Check it out at www.vocabula.com/vocabulareview.htm

ORGANIZATIONS

American Educational Research Association
    1230 17th Street, NW
    Washington, D.C. 20036-3078
    Phone: 202-223-9485
    Web: www.aera.net

International Reading Association
    Headquarters Office
    800 Barksdale Rd.
    PO Box 8139
    Newark, Delaware 19714-8139
    Phone: 302-731-1600
    Web: www.reading.org

National Education Association
    1201 16th Street, NW
    Washington, D.C. 20036-3290
    Phone: 202-833-4000
    Web: www.nea.org

National Reading Conference
    11 East Hubbard Street, Suite 5A
    Chicago, Illinois 60611
    Phone: 312-431-0013
    Web: nrc.oakland.edu
    E-mail: nrc@smtp.bmai.com